Last Match

When Worlds Collide

Mike Box

The Last Match
www.LastMatch.ca
Copyright © 2017 Mike Box
ISBN: 978-1-77277-167-1

Publisher
10-10-10 Publishing
Markham, ON
Canada

Printed in Canada and the United States of America

Contents

Dedication

To my son, Logan, and supporting family and friends, as well as the community.

I am about to become a father to a beautiful baby boy, Logan Christian Xavier, whom I am excited to watch grow into a far greater man than I could have ever been. With the guidance I can bestow upon him, I wish him a bright and pleasant future, as well as the knowledge to overcome all obstacles that are laid before him, with an open mind. My accomplishments allow him the opportunity to grow as an individual, to know he is no better or no worse, to understand and know the value of time, and to know that his mother and I will always love him.

I believe anything is possible with determination and perseverance. Even though every man, woman, and child can have struggles through their lives, we can overcome anything with hope and a dream of a better tomorrow.

For time is of the essence, and it pushes us to strive to accomplish all that we wish to achieve.

To change tomorrow, we must change today.

For all can change in a blink of an eye. Although I hate the struggle that is laid before me, I embrace the knowledge that I have gained.

To live one day is to die another. Immortality is not to live forever, but to be remembered for the things you do.

People are afraid of change, bad or good, but how you deal with both makes the biggest difference about whether to run or face your choices.

To lift or bury, you must see the yin and the yang.

Acknowledgements

A million thanks to...

Presidents Choice Children's Charity
Easter Seals
Sick Kids® - The Hospital for Sick Children
Toronto Rehabilitation Institute Lyndhurst Centre
Bloorview Kids Rehab
Shoppers Home Health Care, Toronto
Holiday Inn, Oshawa
Kinsmen Club, Oshawa
Tim Hortons owners, Anne and Jim
Oshawa Fire Services
Rona, Whitby
Rogers, DDP Studios, and the volunteers for the Million Dollar
Makeover Show
Schools that held fundraisers
Joe Millage
Jordan Veinot and the Polar Bear Swim organizers
Gail and Melissa, who organized Mike's Valentine's Day Dance
Starlight Starbright Foundation
Breath of Light Yoga, and Dawn Pittens
Oshawa Golf and Country Club
Family, friends, and strangers who made donations
to Michael's trust account
Raymond Aaron
Tracy Knepple

Foreword

Mike Box has overcome much in his young life, and he will continue to be challenged for the rest of his journey. However, in spite of his challenges, Mike is thriving and creating an amazing life, with a family he loves and work he enjoys. You will be impressed, moved and inspired by the wonderful story of this young man's amazing journey to independence and purpose.

In *Last Match: When Worlds Collide,* Mike shares his story of what started as an average day at a sporting event, but ended with him fighting for his life. This book is not a tale of his injury, however, but a truly inspirational story of how he rebuilt his world after such a life-altering event. It is the story of how he, as a young man, overcame depression and found his purpose. You will be inspired by the outpouring from his community, which allowed him to finally come home.

If you are facing an obstacle in your life that seems too big to overcome, I challenge you to read this book. You will discover that there is no obstacle too big, no challenge too large, and no event that can take away your ability to define your future and choose your destiny.

Raymond Aaron
New York Times Bestselling Author

Chapter One

Before the Great Divide

The universe has a way of throwing curve balls into your life, ones that can bring amazing personal growth, but not before you endure and overcome. My life is defined by one of the biggest events that could ever happen to someone. It changed how I was going to interact in the world for the rest of my life and it would test my own will to survive.

While most individuals have a few moments where they can point and say, "That was a big change," I can honestly say that my big change was as dramatic as the Grand Canyon. It was a divide, a sharp line in my life, where I could see the before and after—truly what could be referred to as a defining moment.

As teenagers, defining moments aren't usually something we think of. Most of us are thinking about the next meal, the next game, or the next test. We leave home to run to a friend's house or turn around and burrow in the basement with video games and snacks. This is not the time in life where big consequences or life-altering events are supposed to occur. A few bumps and bruises, but nothing that we can't quickly bounce back from.

We learn our coping skills by surviving those minor moments, cutting our teeth on kid-sized problems, not adult ones. Those big defining moments are for adults only and the real world, which we aren't a part of yet. At least, that's what most of us think as teenagers.

So, I didn't know that the day I walked away from my home to attend my last wrestling tournament, I might never walk back in. I was 15 and invincible. Aren't we all at 15? I was a popular kid in my school, well known for my funny, wise-cracking personality as much as my athletic ability. I was a gold medalist in taekwondo. Wrestling was my high school sport, and I won a lot.

Active is probably the best word to describe me. I was jumping, running, skateboarding, and taking life on as only a 15-year-old can. There were no limits to what I was capable of. But it was also important to me to stand up for the little guy. Most of the fights I got into were not for myself but because I was defending someone else.

But I also struggled with learning disabilities. When I was seven, it was determined that I was having trouble with reading, writing, spelling, and my fine motor skills. Back then, I was easily frustrated, but there was something inside of me that was motivated to succeed. From an early age, it was clear that I was going to have challenges in getting my education, but with the right learning plan, I was able to progress in school. I might not have been the valedictorian, but I was still able to contribute, grow, and learn. This early challenge gave me some key coping skills, which I ended up relying on throughout the later years of my life. It also primed my motivation to succeed, another key to my ability to survive the trauma I was going to endure at 15.

Being the funny and athletic guy that I was, I couldn't help but find a girlfriend. In fact, I was looking for my first job and getting ready to sign up for boxing, the next sport I wanted to conquer. I was ambitious, believing there wasn't anything that I couldn't do. In that aspect, I haven't been proven wrong yet! It was truly an easy type of life, with everything going my way.

Of course, there had been one or two bumps in the road that no one ever anticipates. My parents, after having four kids together, separated, and each remarried. The remarriages added more kids to the brood, so all in total, there are 10 of us. We have merged and meshed with each other but, naturally, at 15, I was closest to my full siblings. I think that had a lot to do with being close in age and having gone through a lot of mess together, which seems to come with divorce. My youngest sister hadn't even been born yet when I left for my last wrestling tournament.

There are realities in a family melding and merging that impact your sense of who you are. For me, I received the ability to roll with change. While it might not have always felt the most stable in all stages of my childhood, I also knew that even the worst changes would eventually result in more change, some of which might turn out to be better than before. Sometimes it was just about being patient and waiting it out. However, there are experiences with a greater impact, and those often result in changes that set you on a new life path, one you might never have expected.

My parents loved us but didn't always get along with each other; hence, this was one of many reasons why they got divorced. Get-togethers could be touchy, to say the least. But somehow, we learned to make it work. I regularly saw both my parents and had strong relationships with them both.

I had ended up living with my dad, but I still had regular visits with my mom. She always sees us as the babies we once were, no matter how big we have gotten, or the fact that we are earning our own living or even having children of our own. The privilege of motherhood is that permanent vision of our lives as they were in the beginning.

My dad, on the other hand, believed that we could conquer anything; we just needed to toughen up or muscle our way through. He didn't see babies; he saw the potential we had to be amazing adults.

The day of that particular wrestling tournament in early December 2007, I hadn't been feeling well. I really didn't want to go, but my dad just told me to go out there and win a medal. He was tough on us, mostly to motivate us and make sure we didn't quit. If there was one thing I knew from my dad, it was that quitting wasn't an option.

There was also a dance that night, so I am sure he was thinking that if I was well enough to go to the dance, then I was well enough to wrestle. Plus, let's face it, as a 15-year-old, who wants to miss a chance to dance with your girlfriend and hang out with your buddies? My social life was everything to me, and I wasn't going to miss out on anything unless I was dying or grounded.

So I went to the tournament, but I was running late. Naturally, this meant that I missed the bus. At 15, I wasn't able to just hop in my car and drive over to join my team. But it just so happened that a neighbor saw me walking back home and offered me a ride to the tournament. All those moments that should have kept me away, but each one was conquered by someone with good intentions.

The tournament that changed my life was one that I should have never attended. I often wonder why everything fell into place like it did, and why I had to be the one to go through this dramatic physical event. Why did my life have to be turned upside down? I can't say that I have ever found an answer that is completely satisfactory, but I suspect that someone, somewhere, knew I was strong enough to take these circumstances and survive. Maybe another kid wouldn't have been tough enough, so it had to be me.

Or maybe I was just in the wrong place at the wrong time. I guess I will never know, but my heart and head can't stop musing about it from time to time. Let's just say, if the universe had a message for me that day, the connection wasn't very clear.

Last Match

The message of the universe was mixed to say the least, but what I learned over the course of the next few months, and years, would impact my view of the world in a way that most young people never experience. While I was about to start down a hard road, I was going to learn about how strong I really was and a lot about the good in humanity and the grace that we can find in the most devastating of situations.

Chapter Two

The Line Goes Flat

When I arrived, I immediately got with my team and got to work. That meant warming up, stretching, and finding out who I was going up against first. These tournaments generally worked on a process of elimination, so the better you did, the higher you went in the rounds.

Normally, however, you can only be assigned four matches, but that day I got five. My number was 13; although it was unlucky, it was the hand I was dealt, and I had to fight with it. I just pinned on my number and got ready to kick butt. That day, I guess it turned out to be really true and not just some crazy superstition.

From the loud speaker, every time they called my number that day, it was "Unlucky 13, up to fight!" In my first match, I lost in the second round and dislocated my shoulder (although I didn't know that at the time) when my opponent pinned me to the mat and I tried to break out of it. Thankfully, Serenity was there to massage my shoulder during the breaks between matches. I really just thought that I had to push through the pain. I would be fine later but, right now, I had to win.

Later, my doctor stated that if I had been appropriately examined, it was unlikely that I would have been allowed to compete in my second match. He also noted that my performance was likely hampered by my shoulder injury. It was also determined that I had fractured my shoulder, not just dislocated it. If that had been caught, it is unlikely that the rest of what occurred would have taken place, but those contrary signs from the universe seemed to step into play again.

The assistant coach was with me more that day because the head coach was in another gym with members of my team who were in a higher weight class. This meant that I didn't have the more experienced coach attending my injury, so the telltale signs that might have got me benched for the rest of the tournament weren't caught. Hindsight is always 20/20, no matter what the situation is.

The second match went to me, and my third match didn't show up, so I only had two left and a 45-minute lunch break. I went to my coach and asked for help with my bout sheet because I was having a hard time with it. At the same time, we talked about defenses I could use with my shoulder, which hurt, but I thought wasn't too bad. I was confident I could finish the last two matches.

I won my fourth match and prepared to head to my fifth. It was during this match that I lost and broke my neck in the second round. The details of these few moments are fuzzy because it literally happened so fast.

I remember lining up to start, and then the next thing I knew, I couldn't move. At this point, most of what I know and remember was as I was fading in and out of consciousness, lying on the mat. I remember my coach asking me if I could get up. I replied that I couldn't fucking move. Matches were still going on while I was having seizures and my body was struggling to survive. The coaches and personnel were calling for an ambulance, and someone was contacting my dad.

I can only imagine how scared everyone was, but they kept the matches going. I imagine it was more for the other kids, to keep them from freaking out about me and if I was going to be alright. Nobody ever thought to call my girlfriend that day, so she was left to find out during what was supposed to be one of her fond memories of her high school dances.

The dance had already started; my girlfriend was there, hanging out as only teenage girls can with their friends. We had only just started dating a few months prior to the tournament. I don't think she was even worried about me because she knew wrestling tournaments could take longer than planned.

Plus, it was our first semi-formal and, in the early days of any teenage romance, every first was a big deal! It wasn't until the gossip from the tournament started filtering back to those kids with phones in the gym that she knew what had happened. I imagine she might have thought I stood her up at one point. That night was an emotional roller-coaster for her; she really had no idea what was going on, and my family wasn't reaching out to let her know anything in those first few days. She was left to figure out what had happened from friends who had been there and from the newspapers—not a great situation at all.

Once word got out around the dance, people were standing around crying. No one was sure what was happening and what it meant for me. They just knew a friend was seriously hurt. Our teenage immortality had been broken. Semi-formal was memorable but not for reasons that most people would hope for. The news of my accident ruined the dance for a lot of people. Plus, I never did get to dance with my girlfriend. In fact, I never got to dance again.

In those first moments after my accident, however, I would have given anything just to stand, let alone dance with my girlfriend.

My father was notified and the paramedics took me to Ajax, which was a local hospital. They immediately knew the best place for me was Sick Kids, and I was airlifted there before my mom even got to see me. The Sick Kids hospital staff were fantastic but, for the next few months,

I was fighting with my body. I couldn't feel anything below my chest, and I wasn't sure if I would ever walk again. But even more than that, no one was sure that I was going to live.

My body was broken, and I suffered cardiac arrest multiple times. Everything inside my young frame was going haywire. My brain couldn't effectively talk to the rest of my body, and that was just the beginning.

There was then my deflated lung and the paralyzed right side of my diaphragm. It made breathing so incredibly difficult. At one point, they had to use a ventilator on me, just to make sure I was getting enough oxygen. My neck was in a halo, and I was getting infections over and over again, not to mention the pneumonia.

My skin, my lungs, and all my organs seemed to suffer damage. I was vulnerable to everything, from viruses to bacterial infections. My immune system seemed to almost stop for periods of time. My young body's reserves were quickly spent. Everything was a fight just to stay here with my family and those who loved me so much.

Dad (Scott)

I am a hard worker. It's something I hope that I have passed on to all my children, although Mike probably demonstrated that quality the most. No matter what he put his mind to, he was willing to work to succeed. For Mike, failure wasn't an option.

When I told him to go win a medal, it wasn't just off the cuff. I knew my son, and I expected that he would bring home a sweaty uniform and a medal. I was proud of him. After all, you see so many kids go south after their parents break up, but Mike rises to challenges. He was active, but it wasn't just physically. His mind was always in motion and I could see him doing big things in his future, even if he had moments where he was more focused on having a good time with his buddies.

He had struggled in school, but things seemed to be on track at last. He might not have been geared for an office, but I had every confidence that he would find his path.

The day of the tournament, I was at work. I enjoyed seeing my son wrestle but, with such a large family, work had to come first. At my plant that day, I was on the loader. Partway through my shift, my boss came out to my loader and told me I had a call from Mike's school. It was unusual, and I couldn't imagine why they would be calling. Mike didn't cause trouble, even when he lost, so my only thought was that he must have twisted his ankle or jammed his shoulder, and they needed me to come get him.

I was not prepared to hear that Mike had been injured, and it was severe. They needed me to come right away and told me that he was on his way to the local hospital, which I learned was Ajax. I still didn't think it was more serious than a broken arm.

This was my healthy and vibrant son. I had just seen him earlier in the day. That image of nothing being seriously wrong was shattered by a call from the emergency room doctor a short time later. They wanted to know how far away I was. I asked them what was going on; their lack of a response told me it was going to be really bad.

I remember calling 911 after I got off the phone with the doctor; I told them I was going to be speeding to get to my son, who had been in an accident. Of course, they said that they didn't condone it, but I just said ok and hung up. Then I floored it! I was not close to the hospital, but I made it there in 45 minutes, going about 180 kms.

I pulled up in the emergency room parking and left my car running where the ambulances came in. As I ran up to the door, I saw a priest and doctor waiting for me. In those first moments, they told me that Life Flight was on its way, and the medical staff were trying to stabilize him. Stabilize him?!

My mind started going in a hundred different directions, but then I could hear Mike calling me. Everything crystalized on answering my son. I told them the rest of the explanations would have to wait, and I went into the room where Mike was lying.

I can remember bits and pieces of those first moments. There was the neck brace and Mike saying that he couldn't feel his legs. I was on his left side, and I just kept telling him that everything was going to be okay and that the medical staff was going to make him better. I knew he was scared and, like any parent, I wanted to shield him from the worst. I could see his neck was broken, but I still didn't understand how bad it really was. Even later, when I was told all the details, my brain and heart just couldn't wrap around what I was hearing—not even when the line went flat and monitors started going off.

Medical personnel were racing around, including members of the Life Flight team. The code blue alarm was going off, signaling this intense dance between life and death with the medical personnel fighting for Mike's life. Later, I learned that he had a massive heart attack. I was shoved out of the way because they needed to make room for the machines and critical personnel.

Those moments in the hallway, watching them attempt to revive Mike, were some of the longest in my life. I couldn't imagine that my son would only be in my life for just 15 years. My heart and head were just frozen as Mike hovered between life and death. The goal of the team was to stabilize him long enough for the trip to Sick Kids, which could provide the specialized treatment that Mike was going to need.

At some point, I know I made a few key calls to Mike's grandfather and my wife. I tried calling his mother but didn't get a hold of her right away. When she called me back, I gave her a quick summary of what had happened and where we were headed. She would have to meet us at Sick Kids because she would never make it to Ajax before we left. When Mike was stabilized, they loaded him into a helicopter and handed me a helmet. I was in the helicopter, and we were off. While I was in the helicopter, everyone else was on their way to Sick Kids, driving as fast as they could.

Even in the helicopter, Mike's condition continued to deteriorate. I remember hearing them yell that we were 7 minutes to the roof top of Sick Kids. That was one of the longest flights of my life as we hovered in the air, and Mike hovered between life and death.

Once we got to Sick Kids, the fight for Mike continued. He kept flatlining, and they needed to give him a breathing and feeding tube. While at Ajax, and throughout the journey to Sick Kids, I kept talking to Mike, telling him not to give up. This was the moment where I needed the fighter in Mike to rise up.

I didn't want to have to tell his mother and his siblings that he had left us. I just kept telling him that I wasn't giving up on him, and he couldn't give up on me. He couldn't die on me. It was the beginning of a long period where I refused to dwell on anything but Mike's survival. I didn't worry about my own feelings or needs. Everything was focused around my son.

Jewel, my wife at the time, joined me at Sick Kids. When I told her what was going on, I recognized that I was in shock, but I didn't have time to worry about myself. I had to be strong for my son. Little did I realize how much of a toll that this fight was going to take on me and those in my family that I loved so much.

The breathing tube turned out to be counter-productive because Mike had fluid building up in his lungs. Basically, he was drowning himself. They considered doing a tracheotomy, but I talked them into pulling the breathing tube instead. Mike started breathing again after that and, fortunately, he never did have a tracheotomy.

Week after week, I was by my son's side. But this was a stressful time. My relationship with my ex-wife wasn't the greatest, and it got worse during this time. She had the added stress from her pregnancy, on top of Mike's condition, and her own fears for his life. Her family's history made this evening more painful, but I'll let her tell you about that.

Mike had surgery and there was a constant stream of meetings about his condition and what we could expect in terms of his recovery. My vibrant son was not likely to walk again, and they couldn't really tell us what his future was going to look like. I didn't know if my son would ever be able to live on his own, let alone have a career or a family. We didn't know if he would still be Mike after all of this, or if his brain was going to give up, or if his wonderful personality was going to disappear.

Throughout the first 8 weeks that Mike was in the hospital, it was difficult to fully understand what was happening from day to day. I didn't want to think about what the future was going to look like, especially when I wasn't even sure if he was going to live to the next day. The drugs he was on were so powerful that he would swear he saw demons in his room, among other things. Then there were the continual flat lines and close calls. My heart broke to see him struggling so hard just to stay with us. But I also knew that without our support, he would never make it.

One such experience stands out to me; it was another heart attack like the one Mike had at Ajax. I had just woken up and went to see him in his room. All the tubes were out and Mike asked if I wanted to watch a movie with him. It was a form of escape from the reality of our situation and a break we definitely needed. I agreed but told him I was going to go out for a smoke first and that I would be right back.

I got to the elevator, but I couldn't get on when the doors opened on two women, one a nurse and the other a lady in civilian clothing. I just knew I had to get back to his room. As soon as I walked back in, he said something wasn't right. The next moment, he crashed.

The nurses called another code blue, and this one was even more severe than anything before. They were using the paddles on Mike, but he wasn't responding. The doctor even looked at me and told me that it wasn't likely that Mike was coming back. I refused to believe that my son was leaving me. But the doctor said, "We have paddled him twice and he isn't responding."

"No, no, no, he is coming back!" I said as I ran around the bed. I started whispering into Mike's ear that he couldn't give up on me. I kept talking, sure that Mike could hear me. The doctor saw Mike start to respond, and encouraged me to keep talking. Mike was considered clinically dead for 5 minutes; the doctor was ready to give up, but I wasn't, and Mike clearly wasn't either!

Later, when Mike woke up, he said he heard my voice in the void. I called him back to me and he asked me about acne cream, which he was sure that I would forget to put on him. What a thing for him to think of! But I knew our connection was still strong enough that he wasn't ready to give up and leave us. For that, I was extremely grateful.

I knew there was always a possibility back then that my voice would no longer call Mike back and that he could end up leaving us for good. I didn't want to dwell on it, but it was always looming in the back of my mind during those first few months in the hospital.

The experiences we had in the hospital revolved around Mike's off the wall comments and questions. Between the drugs and the injuries, plus all the infections and issues that his body had to deal with, it was sometimes like dealing with someone who had drank too much or was slightly off the deep end.

One of those periods was when he got it into his head that the nurses were ripping him off and not letting him have his orange juice. For some reason, he became obsessed with orange juice, sure that it was the only thing that would cure his thirst. In fact, he was sure that a refrigerator full of medicine was actually full of orange juice, which the nurses weren't giving him. He wasn't very pleasant during this period because he wanted something and couldn't have it.

Still, the nurses didn't take it personally, and they gave him extraordinary care. In fact, if it weren't for them taking such an active interest in him, I am not sure that he would have made it. They didn't just nurse his body—they also nursed his spirit.

Throughout the weeks at Sick Kids, the staff did what they could to accommodate our family. I had split visits with Mike's mom. Christmas Day was truly a family affair. Members of the community and local businesses made sure that we had presents, and the staff at the hospital got us a large private room, which allowed the family to gather and spend the day with Mike. I felt the love of our community during this stressful time for our family, but it was just the beginning of the outreach from our hometown.

Still, the stress and overwhelming fear that I had been pushing down eventually found its way out. I couldn't keep it bottled up forever. Christmas evening, I stepped across the street from the hospital and found a local drug store. I remember asking for some drugs to help me sleep. Up until that moment, I hadn't shed a tear or showed any real emotion beyond frustration and angry spats with my ex-wife.

In that drug store, though, the emotion welled up and I burst into tears. Individuals tried to help me, but I just needed to release all those emotions. The reality of my son's new life and how his world had changed just kept hitting me at odd times over the next few years. Adjusting to Mike's new life was going to be a family affair, but we wouldn't be the same family a few years later.

Mom (Loretta)

The day that was the beginning of a mother's nightmare actually started out fairly normal. I was eight months pregnant, which meant I was up to weekly doctor's visits. In fact, when I got the news, I was at the doctor's office. The receptionist received a call for me, then walked over and gave me a message that I needed to call my father right away. I had no idea why my dad would be calling me, but I wasn't alarmed.

The receptionist offered up one of the exam rooms so that I could use the phone in relative privacy. I called my father and he said that Scott was trying to get ahold of me because something had happened to Michael. I tried calling Scott, but the line was busy.

I walked out to the waiting room and told my husband, Gary, that something had happened to Michael. I think he was trying to make sure I didn't worry, so he said something to the effect that he probably just broke his arm or something, so don't stress. We knew Michael had a wrestling tournament and he was a bit of a daredevil. But something made me turn to Gary and say, "But he could have broken his neck."

I went back in the room and tried to call Scott again. This time, he answered. He told me he was at Ajax hospital, but that they were airlifting Michael to Sick Kids because he was in serious condition with a broken neck and had already flatlined. I really don't remember if I was still holding the phone when the doctor came in, but I do remember that I was crying and telling her that I needed to go. She told me that she needed to take my blood pressure because she was afraid that it would be extremely high because of the stress.

They finally let me go, but I know that they had to be worried about me and my little one. I was just focused on getting to Mike.

Gary and I left the doctor's office and began the long drive to Sick Kids in Toronto. I was crying the whole time and praying for my son. My baby was hurt, and I was so far away. As a mother, it is a helpless feeling that no one can truly imagine until they are in the situation. It is a feeling I wouldn't wish on anyone. The drive, which felt like forever, finally ended as we reached the parking lot.

I found out where he was and we were brought to his room in the trauma unit. There were three people there who were waiting to walk us through what we were about to see. One of the individuals told us that we couldn't appear upset, because he would get upset, and they had just gotten him comfortable.

The view of my son that first time was a shock. There were machines everywhere and monitors beeping constantly. Within the room, there were so many people. It seemed as if there wasn't a free spot anywhere, but I was able to walk up to Michael and tell him I loved him and that everything would be okay.

What mother doesn't want to reassure her child that he will be alright? My own brain was reeling from the possible outcomes and what this could mean for his future. I still don't think it was truly real to me at this point. I was still in a state of shock. It was during this conversation that Michael told me he couldn't feel his body, which meant that it was much worse than just a broken neck.

Next thing I knew, we were being ushered out so they could take him to surgery. The hospital provided us with a trauma counsellor who took us into a room to wait and walked us through what was taking place and what to expect in the next few hours. That was the longest night of my life. The waiting area where we were at had small rooms so you could lay down and try to get some sleep. I don't think any of us could sleep during that wait. When Michael was brought into recovery, we got to see him.

He was lying so peacefully, but it was even scarier for me because, now in addition to all the machines, he had this tremendous halo on his head, holding his neck in place where it had broken.

For the next few weeks, the news from the hospital staff, about Michael's condition, would be up and down. During that first visit in recovery, we were told that Michael's right lung had collapsed and it was filling up with fluid. Touch and go was an understatement for the next few weeks. But at that moment, he was stable, and we felt it was safe to go home, get cleaned up, and start telling the family.

I didn't have to tell the children that I had with Scott because he had already broken the news to them. My own family was devastated at the news, and we spent the rest of the day making arrangements to be there for Michael.

My family filled the waiting room that day and into the evening. I remember walking in and flashing back to when my own brother had been shot. He had been so young, and the loss was something that my family had never fully recovered from. I know the grief of that loss is something my mother still carries to this day. It never goes away but just takes up residence in your heart.

The waiting room had been filled with family then too, but now they were all praying for Michael to recover and pull through after this horrific accident. But a thought crossed my mind that they might think they were there to tell him good-bye. I wasn't ready to do that, so I *just stopped myself from even thinking that way. I couldn't think that way, not if Mike had a chance to survive. He needed us to all believe and be pulling for him.*

Our family's tragedy was compounded, as my own father ended up having a stroke later that day. He already suffered from heart problems and I honestly think the stress was just too much for him.

But the stress also caused some pretty heated moments between Scott and myself. Our spouses were naturally involved as well, backing each of us to the hilt. The arguments brought up old wounds about how each of us parented and harkened back to our marriage's low points. At one point, it got so bad that we were told that we would all be kicked out and given different times and days with Michael. The hospital staff was no longer willing to serve as referees for us. You would think that we would have managed to stop and take control of ourselves at that point. But we just couldn't seem to manage to step beyond our differences, even in this horrible situation.

There is a toll that divorce and trauma take on a family, and it can cause rifts that you would never expect, as everyone deals with the shock and horror of the situation. Plus, we were all trying to process what this was going to mean for Michael and the rest of us. Old wounds get reopened, and you find that what you thought you had made your peace with was actually just lurking under the surface, ready to leap out and ambush you.

There is so much stress while watching your child fight for his life and there not being anything you can do about it. Plus, I was worried about the little life inside of me, whom I was trying to keep in just a little longer for her own sake.

I watched them come in and drain tubes that were keeping his lungs clear, not to mention the feeding tube and the screws that were holding his halo onto his head and body. The screws left little scars in his forehead, which you can still find if you know where to look.

But I knew he was fighting to stay alive. I could see it in his eyes. One of the best days was when he woke up and was able to talk. You never realize how much an "I love you" means until you hear it from your child after such a horrific event.

The biggest fight, apart from the physical for Michael, was depression. There were days when he said, "I just want to die. I can't live this way." I kept telling him that I couldn't lose him; I needed him to live. I had lived through the grief my parents felt when they buried my brother, and I didn't want to be in their shoes. I was determined not to bury my son. History wasn't going to repeat itself.

Then there were the papers to deal with. Scott had called them and the story was getting out to our community. I am a private person, so I didn't have much to say. But our community started rallying around our family, and donations started coming in to help with Michael. We didn't know what the future was going to be for him, but their help was appreciated as Scott and I took it day by day.

Thanks to my condition, Scott ended up taking point more often during the first few weeks. I physically couldn't handle being there as much as he could. Plus, I had doctors concerned for my health and that of my baby.

My doctor was especially concerned about my elevated blood pressure, so that is when they imposed every other day visits on me. The doctor was concerned for the baby and me, but my mind was focused on Michael, and it was hard for me as a mother to divide myself. After all, I had other children to care for and think about, plus Michael and the baby.

As a parent, I was stretched thin, but mothers all over the world know how hard it is for us to stop and care for ourselves when we feel the pull of our families' needs. I think I was more stressed having to wait for my visit day with Michael then I was when I was actually up there with him.

The day Gary decided to paint the baby's room, my mother drove me up to see Michael. I remember walking in and seeing Scott and the counselor waiting for me. My throat dropped into my stomach; I shook my head as tears filled my eyes. I was sure they had bad news for me and I didn't want to hear it.

The counselor took me to a private room and told me that Michael was stable now, but he had needed to be revived yet again. Then, a horrible pain shot through my stomach; I jumped up and then bent over. I didn't want anyone to touch me. At that moment, all I wanted was to be left alone to cry.

The counselor could see that I needed to be checked out. She ran out to get a nurse. They determined that I needed to go to the hospital across the street; I think they realized that Hailey might be ready to make an appearance. But I wouldn't go without seeing Michael first. My mother called Gary to tell him where I was headed, but they saw I wasn't going to go until I saw Michael. My son got his stubbornness from both his parents; that was for sure! So they took me to his room, just to pacify me, but it was worth standing firm.

I think in my heart, I was afraid that, if I left, I wouldn't ever see him alive again. But if I saw him, then I could tell him to hang on until I got back.

When we entered the room, he wasn't in the first bed like before. As I was wheeled in, they explained he had been moved to the next bed area. Standing by him was a priest praying, and my mind immediately went to the worst. I screamed, "NO!" and started to pull myself out of the wheelchair to run over to my son. The priest and nurse immediately reassured me that he was ok and that the priest was just there to pray for healing. That was an image burnt into my head that I will never forget.

I told Michael I loved him and that I would be back. Then they wheeled me through a tunnel to the other hospital. The checkup confirmed what my doctor had feared; the stress was having a negative impact on my pregnancy. The baby had dropped and I was dilated 3 centimeters, yet it wasn't even Christmas; she was due January 12th of 2008. I couldn't leave Michael though, even after being encouraged to go home and rest.

After being checked out, I went back to his room to make sure he was comfortable. The doctors outside of his room were talking to me, but I can't remember what they said. It was like watching lips move with no sound. Still in shock that I had almost lost my son, I couldn't process anything that they said that day. All I could think was that Michael had to be okay.

Mike

One moment that I remember from those early days in the hospital was a feeling of having left my body. I was staring down at myself and I could see all the machines beeping around me. Across from me was this woman, and she kept telling me that they were going to slit my throat.

Now I realize that they were getting ready to do a tracheotomy but, back then, I had no idea what that might have meant. I wasn't fearful of that idea because I felt so peaceful floating above myself. It was surreal and gave me a feeling of grace, as if some higher presence wanted me to feel some measure of comfort.

As I slipped back into my body, I didn't realize that I was not breathing. My father was encouraging them to pull the tubes out of my throat instead of allowing them to do a tracheotomy, because he was sure that was the reason I couldn't breathe. Again, against their better judgment—at least I imagine they thought it was a bad idea—they pulled the tubes. Surprisingly, my dad was right, and I started breathing on my own. So, they didn't end up having to slit my throat, so to speak, but it was one of many close calls.

I don't remember much of the first weeks in the hospital. I was kept medicated for a variety of reasons, plus my injuries and the infections kept me fading in and out of consciousness. I would have moments when I talked with my family, but I don't remember now things that I said or even mentioned to them. When my dad talks about the orange juice, I mostly draw a blank.

I wish I could have kept that feeling of peace from my out of body experience with me constantly, but the realities of my condition didn't allow for me to always have peace of mind. In fact, my mind was full of turmoil as I tried to determine who I was now. It seemed as if most of the descriptions that I came up with started and ended with my physical limitations because, at that point in my journey, it was all I could see.

Nothing else seemed to matter because I couldn't get up and walk on my own. A moment on a mat had ended my life, and I wasn't sure how I was ever going to get it back. A 15-year-old brain can't see much past the moment, and I definitely demonstrated that during the first months after my injury.

Keep in mind, I was an extremely active teenager who had done everything for myself. Now, I had to have someone help me with everything, from going to the bathroom to eating. It was embarrassing to me for strangers to see me in this vulnerable state. Plus, I had no idea if it would ever change. There were no guarantees that I would regain any function or movement, based on how high up my injury was. The doctors were taking a "wait and see" attitude, while they let my body heal. I think everyone was hoping my young body would produce a miracle, but that wasn't to be.

Not only was I dealing with the reality that I might never be able to get along without help from strangers again, I was processing what that meant for the rest of my life. It is a lot for a young man to take in. Ambitious, with goals and dreams— that was me. Now I had to try to figure out what was going to be possible and how I was going to move forward. My family rallied around me, but it had a significant impact on both my parents, my step-parents at the time, and my siblings.

Then, there was the reality that I might never be alone again. To never have any privacy, that is the kiss of death to a teenager who has spent the last few years fighting to get privacy from their parents, siblings, and the world in general.

Stress and depression were two huge parts of our lives for those first few months. Not only did I have this new reality to contend with, my girlfriend and I had broken up by the time I returned from rehab. She was only 15 at the time of the accident, and the idea of sticking by me was overwhelming. I had given her a choice and, unfortunately, her choice was to move on. I couldn't even fight for her because I was fighting for my life and my future. I was dealing with so many challenges and this was just one I couldn't take on. I was having a hard-enough time facing reality, because reality, at that point, was just brutal.

I was battling depression, and my parents were stressed and overwhelmed. They kept taking it out on each other and they ended up with separate visiting hours and visiting days. On top of it all, my mom was pregnant with my little sister, Hailey. The stress was so bad that on doctor's orders, she could only visit me every other day. They were hoping that by limiting her visits, they could keep her from having my sister too early.

But it was not to be. She came a few weeks early, on December 26, but thankfully, she was healthy. My mom now had the work of a newborn and supporting me. I know there were moments when I felt like a burden, and I wondered if it wouldn't be better to just slip away. Depression can play funny tricks on your head, making you see life as not worth living, even when there is yet so much to do and explore.

Mom (Loretta)

That first Christmas was just a few weeks after the accident. Our family was determined to include Michael and make it the family holiday that it would have been at home.

The hospital put Michael in a private room for the day. Scott went up in the morning and I went up that afternoon. Both of us were with him for part of the day, and my mom went up to see him for the evening, so Michael wasn't alone at all that first Christmas.

Hailey came the next day. I remember giving my name, and this horrible feeling came over me because they all knew that I was Michael's mother, the boy who had been injured in the wrestling accident. They were kind, but all the staff kept asking about Michael and how he was doing. It was more stress, and I kept thinking that I was trying to give life to this new child as my son was fighting for his own. Even the TV had a Sick Kids hospital marathon on, which meant there was no escape from the reminders about Michael.

I only stayed in the hospital one night, but I made sure that they took Michael a picture of his new sister and hung it on his wall. As soon as I was released, I went right to Sick Kids to see Michael. I couldn't take the baby in to see him, but Michael wanted to see her. He was talking by then and, after a few up and down alternating visits between myself and Gary, the nurses surprised us by putting Michael in a private room. Finally, he could meet his baby sister, and that is another memory that I was grateful to have.

Mike

The first Christmas after my injury, my family came up and celebrated with me. Donations from the community had come pouring in, with funds for my parents to travel and, eventually, funds that would allow my father's home to be retrofitted to accommodate my wheelchair and all the space that I would need. More about that later. After months at Sick Kids, where I was stabilized and received surgery to fuse two of my vertebrae together, it was time to head to rehab.

This was where I would find out what type of life quality I could expect and how much independence I might be able to have. But I was also going to learn about my body's new abilities and how to redefine progress considering my diagnosis.

Chapter Three

Working Out for My Future

Rehab was meant to be a sign that I was getting better, but it was also going to be a huge reality check. Whatever feeling I had regained, I hoped would continue to grow. My doctors were less optimistic, but they didn't want me to give up, so they didn't tamper my hopes as much as they could have.

The beginning of rehab was a move to Bloorview Kids Rehab Hospital. It was a sign of hope, in that my body was finally healing and ready to get to work. I was able to give a high five with my right arm and twitch my left arm at that time. It was more than anyone had thought I would have, based on my initial lack of feeling and how high my injury was.

My dad attended the orientation for Bloorview and he was impressed with the facility. I was happy to get a private room. It's hard to rest when the only thing separating you from your roommate is the equivalent of a shower curtain. Plus, the reality of a hospital is that nurses are in and out throughout the night. They have to check vitals, give medications and, in general, do the myriad of tasks they are assigned. For me, that also meant getting turned and moved on a regular basis so that my skin's integrity wouldn't be further compromised.

Needless to say, it's hard to get a good night's sleep in a hospital, and even worse when you can't change position on your own to get comfortable. I was like a toy doll. I could be put in a variety of positions and then just left there. Thankfully, no one thought it would be a good idea to just stick my leg in the air and leave it there. The staff was always trying to make me as comfortable as possible, but it wasn't easy, especially when I couldn't feel pain consistently, or at all.

I had a lot of friends who visited regularly, but it was hard for me to let them see me in my new condition. In February 2008, my friends and schoolmates showed me the true meaning of friendship. They held a fundraiser for me, and it was clear that everyone was grateful to see me when I unexpectedly showed up. My attendance was a surprise for them that night. Hearing how much I was missed gave me a lift I couldn't have anticipated, but desperately needed. So that fundraiser ended up doing more than just raising money. It raised my spirits too!

Still, there were some definite highlights to my time in the hospital and rehab. I had a variety of visitors, more than just family and friends. Some pretty famous people came to root me on in my healing process. One of those visits had to do with the sport of Canadians—hockey!

Members of the Maple Leafs had visited me in the hospital, which was a great experience for any red-blooded Canadian male. Hockey is the national pastime and everyone grew up playing it, even if we aren't all destined for the big leagues. But my pictures from that initial visit had disappeared, which was disappointing. I suspect that someone thought they would be worth money, with all the signatures on them. It's sad but, unfortunately, things like that can happen.

Then, prior to my move to Bloorview, I received a surprising visit from Jason Schwabe, who was the community relations coordinator for the Maple Leafs. He had heard that my pictures had disappeared, so he came up with something to replace those mementos. During his visit, he gave me a limited-edition hockey stick signed by the team, an

Eddie Belfour jersey, and a hat. I still have that stick, and it remains one of my prized possessions.

But with this move to rehab in early January of 2008, I was facing a new reality that I couldn't ignore. This is where life got complicated. When most of us think of rehab, they think of it in terms of regaining motion or a skill that was lost due to an injury or stroke.

By the time I was transferred to rehab, I had regained feeling in my arms and hands to a degree. It was determined that I was paralyzed from the nipples of my chest down. This was better than they had expected because, originally, they had thought I would be paralyzed from the shoulders down. But rehab taught me that there was a lot I could do for myself, even if I only had limited use of my hands.

Technology itself impacted my life in many ways. I have computers that respond to my voice, an electric wheelchair, and multiple devices geared to give me as much freedom as possible. I still need help to get transferred into my wheelchair and from my chair into my bed or another seat, but at least I don't need someone to push me all the time.

Within rehab, I worked hard, both to gain back any movement or function I could, but also to maximize the function and movement I had already regained. I was retraining my body and brain to talk with each other. It was like they were on a blind date after years of talking online. Now, in each other's presence, it was like they had nothing to say to each other!

For me, every ability is a product of that time and hard work. The mental work was just as hard as the physical. At the end of the day, I had to tell myself that I wanted to live and I had to be my own biggest support. Not that I didn't have plenty of people in my corner; I can't say enough about my family and friends, and their support, both then and through the years since.

But my will to survive had to be great enough to fight the depression and the mental anguish that comes with such a dramatic physical change.

Throughout my time in the hospital and rehab, I had a lot of visitors. Friends from school and, of course, my family all came to see me. Nothing can uplift the spirit like seeing the faces of people from your regular life. They would talk about what was going on in the world outside of your hospital room. It gets your mind off what is going on in your life at the moment.

Teenagers are rarely confronted with such a dramatic and life-altering experience. Most of us are focused on things that seem to be such huge emotional events, but the reality is they are just blips on the road, like the end of a first relationship or finding out a crush doesn't know you exist, or getting a C when you expected a B —or other seemingly big deals.

None of that truly prepares someone for a moment when your ability to be an independent individual disappears, or you face your own mortality in such a profound way. Unfortunately, we don't think about building that type of mental strength because, at 15, many of us don't think we need it.

There were also moments of jealousy and envy, when I would see someone just stand up from a sitting position and walk away, knowing that I was unlikely to ever do that again. It was hard not to sink into a negative spiral when that jealousy and envy would rear its head. But I didn't have much time for pity parties at that point because rehab was the most intense work I had ever done in my life.

Remember, I was an active and athletic kid. I could easily do a variety of fitness activities, from sit-ups to pull-ups. It was no problem for me to exert myself physically in a variety of areas. Now, my therapists had to put me into various positions and push me to perform just the smallest of muscle movements.

Then there were the sores. I had multiple pressure sores on my body. In an individual with the ability to move, they naturally turn throughout the night as they sleep. These involuntary movements distribute the pressure of their bodies over all of their skin; one area doesn't take the brunt of all the weight of the body for an extended period. In a quadriplegic, that isn't possible.

My body can't do those simple movements that are necessary to maintain the integrity of your skin. I need others to turn me on a regular basis, but it is no guarantee that the sores won't develop.

While I was at Sick Kids, I was in a coma for a period of time. During that time, I developed these pressure sores. The sores turned into ulcers that had to be cared for to avoid infections. Proper wound care included encouraging my body to heal, but after so much had happened to my body, I didn't have the ability to heal as quickly as I once had. That meant my caretakers had to monitor these sores and make sure they were kept clean and screened for any signs of infection.

My family was learning as well. They had to master caring for me and what would be involved in wound care once I got home. My step-mother just stepped into the breach, and proved to be a pivotal person in my life during my first few months at home.

Dad (Scott)

While Mike was in rehab, his mom, my wife, Jewel, and I had so much to learn about what Mike would be able to do and what he couldn't. I had to take in information about caring for his pressure ulcers, and recognize that he was going to be depending on us for everything when he got home. It was yet one more challenge we had to face.

As a father, I had to stop and recognize how difficult this was for my son to rely on us so completely. At the same time, I had to acknowledge how difficult it was for me to see my son in this helpless state. He couldn't even go to the bathroom without help. I found that I shied away from the care aspects that came with a son who was a quadriplegic. I had exhausted myself in the fight to keep Mike alive and, during rehab, I found myself emotionally and physically spent.

I also had to grieve, which was something that I kept myself from doing for months. Mike was not only my son, he was my prodigy. I saw him following in my footsteps, raising his own family, and being active in his community. He was a great kid and always willing to help anyone who needed something. To be in a position where he had to ask for help on a daily basis wasn't just hard for Mike to swallow, it was hard for me as well.

For parents whose children have lived through such traumatic events, there is definitely a grieving process. As we raise our children, we build up a store of dreams about who they will be, what they will achieve, and how their futures will look. Events like these take all those dreams and aspirations and throw them right out the window. You have to grieve the loss of the person your child used to be and embrace who they are now. It also means creating a new set of hopes and dreams for them. I had to figure out how to be in his corner and what type of support he needed. Some days he would lash out, angry at what had happened. We couldn't blame him. But it was hard not to take it *personally, even though you knew that he wasn't really angry with you, but the situation and his inability to change it.*

It isn't easy. Counseling can be a great tool, but it can be hard to take time for yourself, when you see that your child has a laundry list of their own needs. Then you still have to care for your other children. They need you to parent and guide them, but you can quickly feel as if you are out of resources, thus short-changing someone. That leads to even more guilt, because you can't be a superhero, meeting everyone's needs and caring for your own.

Some days are filled with positive moments; those days help you get through the hard ones. In rehab, at Bloorview, we learned what Mike was going to be able to do but also the long list of things that he wouldn't be able to do for himself anymore. The possibility of him walking again was basically taken off the table. It became about building his muscle strength and teaching him how to capitalize on what his body could accomplish, using a combination of his shoulder muscles and natural reflexes.

We cheered any progress he made, but we recognized that it wasn't likely to result in Mike walking or even standing on his own again. Still, every task he could do for himself gave him back another layer of independence, which was key to him overcoming the waves of depression that occasionally tried to swamp him.

As a parent, I found myself fighting my own depression about the situation, which was compounded by the emotions that I had stuffed for a long period of time. My relationship with my wife also suffered, as the strain of all the demands from Mike's condition and our new reality took its toll. I never doubted my decision to take Mike home, but I also now understand that it was a lot to ask of my wife to take on the burden of caring full-time for him. I didn't recognize her own feelings of being overwhelmed until it was too late.

All of us had mental and emotional anguish that we had to deal with over this situation. Mike's mother and I had to find a way to make peace as we cheered our son on. But at the same time, we all weren't dealing with our own grief. Pushing that off just made us all ticking time bombs, which could go off at any time.

Mike

As I look back at rehab, I realize how much mental energy it took for me to keep moving forward. I was struggling with dark thoughts of depression and anxiety. The doctors even recognized that I was suicidal at various points in my treatment. It was hard not to think that my life wasn't worth anything. When you can move and function as an independent individual, it is easy to take for granted that you will always be able to contribute to society and you will always be able to do what you want. There are no limitations, and you don't imagine that you will ever have to deal with any profound changes in your life. Most of us just assume our life will follow a certain path, and we can adjust it, but the choices are ours to make.

I didn't imagine any limitations because, prior to my accident, there simply weren't any! The world was at my feet, just waiting for me to jump in and explore. My father had pushed me to try anything, and I had the confidence to believe anything was possible. What a way to suddenly learn about limits!

It was a dramatic change of circumstances, and one that left me wondering what I would do with my life now. What good would I be to my family? Would I just be a burden, sitting in a wheelchair waiting to die? What about having a life with a partner or even just being social with my friends? Would anything I had done before be possible now? I survived, but what kind of life was I going to have?

Now I saw my life, not as a blessing, but as a burden on the ones that I loved so much. Rehab was where I started the process of finding out what I could do for myself and rebuilding my independence, such as it was. This was also where I started to reconnect with my life, seeing what was still possible and absorbing the new shape of my future.

Negative thoughts were something to be held at bay, but I also felt under siege from all the bad news that seemed to be coming my way. I didn't stop to grieve for my old life. Instead, I just hid my grief in anger and resentment.

There were moments when I could just pretend my old life hadn't existed, but I couldn't fully embrace where I was until I made my peace with where I had been. And that took time. I can even say that process is one that will never be fully complete, but I am always working toward the goal of peace with my accident and its long-reaching impact.

It was also a constant struggle to focus on what I could do, versus what I couldn't do. I survived, but now I needed to live. I needed to find a way to thrive where I was planted. I had to develop a new outlook to make my life the best it could be. I had to take what the universe had given me and turn it into a life that I could be excited to live and be happy with. But my parents weren't this deep in my head, so I don't know if they understood all of the struggles I was dealing with on a mental and emotional level. I hadn't really started to examine the spirituality of my situation, but it would also be a part of my journey toward a more whole life.

During my stint in rehab, several key things became apparent. First, I was going to need intensive daily care to maintain my skin integrity and general hygiene. It was going to mean more care than my parents could provide on their own. Second, the current layout of my father's home wasn't going to work for me and all the medical equipment I would need just to survive and maintain my general health and well-being.

This brought my family face to face with a huge financial burden, on top of the emotional and mental ones that they were already facing. We weren't a poor family exactly, but we were a large family. My parents both had the general care of their families to consider and they didn't have hundreds of thousands in their savings for an event like this.

My father, who I was living with at the time of my accident, was facing this burden head on. His solution was to sell our family home and buy one that could accommodate me, my wheelchair, and all my other new accessories, even if it meant having to cut the budget somewhere else to afford the new mortgage payment.

Can you imagine the kind of love I felt at his willingness to do whatever it took to bring me home? But there was a lot of guilt too; I knew the family was going through all this because of me. The mind is a funny thing; it isn't as if I had been injured on purpose, but my thoughts ran to a negative vein all the same.

There were times when I couldn't help but wonder why they had fought so hard to keep me alive. Didn't they know that I was going to be a burden? Didn't they know that my quality of life was going to dramatically change? Why would they do that? Looking back, I know now that they didn't care about all of that. They just wanted me to still be there to laugh and joke with them at family events. They still wanted to hear my voice and see me smile. They wanted to be complete as a family and, without me, they wouldn't be.

My own mother's grief at losing her brother meant that she was determined not to lose a son. Both of my parents poured their strength of will into me. I wasn't going to die on them. They were adamant about that. Still, once my health was more stable, the realities of what my injuries meant for the family became crystal clear.

But then something happened that none of us expected. My parents wanted to encourage me through the rehab, but they were also both emotionally spent. My support system needed to recharge its batteries for the road ahead, but there really wasn't time. We were like a car running on empty, trying to get a few more miles out of the tank. Eventually, our car was just going to stop. But then one of those periods of my life, where I felt the presence of something greater than myself, happened. The kindness of others was about to play a part in our lives, as you will soon see.

Chapter Four

It Takes a Village

My hometown was what I would call average by most standards. We had our downtown, shopping, and different local hangouts. There was good food to be had and farms a short drive out. It wasn't huge, but it was a tight-knit community. We helped each other out when there was a need but, mostly, we relied on our families. It was a sense of independence that ran through all of us.

As a fairly self-sufficient young man, I always wanted to help others. It was, and is still, a part of my nature. But to ask for help, well now, that was something different. I could handle anything that came my way, so why would I need anyone to help me?

I am reminded of the saying: let him who thinks he is standing beware that he doesn't fall. I never thought I could fall, but these circumstances taught me that falling, and falling hard, could happen to anyone. Now I needed help, and so did my family. The question was, how could we ask for it? Pride can often make it hard to bend when you need to.

But we found that we didn't have to ask. Our community decided to answer the question we never put to them. They stepped up in a profound way, and it gave my family the financial and, more importantly, the emotional boost that they needed to keep moving forward through my first few months at home.

When I look back, I saw how they served as angels in disguise. In the moments when my family couldn't think about putting another step forward, someone would stop by and help in some way. They were not always big grand gestures, but those small kindnesses meant the world to us. Those small acts of kindness gave us a boost, and they always seemed to happen at just the right time.

Dad (Scott)

The support from the community was overwhelming, especially at a time when we were struggling just to understand what Mike's injury meant in terms of what he could do and couldn't do.

The local Tim Hortons outlet at King Street East and Drew Street had donated money to our family. The Oshawa Holiday Inn donated a room for me to stay in while Mike was in Toronto. Half of the proceeds from a fundraiser, in January 2008, where Ajax residents took a dip in Lake Ontario, went toward a new wheelchair for Mike. A trust fund for Mike was also set up at the Bank of Montreal, where people could donate. The money was then available for Mike's long-term care.

Each of these gestures lifted one burden or another off of my shoulders. It gave my family a sense of peace as we struggled through the fight for Mike's survival, and through the first few months in rehab, as well as all the medical knowledge we had to learn in order to understand what had happened. But it also gave us so much more.

We went from struggling to figure out how we were going to manage the expenses of being with Mike while he was in the hospital and rehab, to having the ability to just focus on Mike, thanks to our community's generosity.

Throughout it all, every single day, the community just wowed us. There were a lot of tough times with layoffs during that period, but the support was overwhelming. The community took care of one of its own, even though they were each dealing with their own problems and challenges.

I saw the beauty of humanity and how kindness can reach across the barriers that we can build among ourselves. It is these moments of kindness that can build an amazing sense of peace and love from a horrible experience. They can also be a way to provide mental and emotional support for a family that is in the depths of despair.

My children also got a lesson in the love of a community and how you can impact another family's life. I have seen my children all become more giving as a result of this experience, so I believe that my community has done something that will be paid forward over the years to come.

Mike

All the publicity of my accident had mobilized our community in a way that we had never expected. First, it was the financial and emotional support they provided to my family during my initial hospital stay at Sick Kids. My parents were able to be there for me because of the financial support of others. They contributed to bank accounts and even had fundraisers to benefit my family during this difficult initial stage of my journey.

However, our larger need was preparing the house for my return from rehab. I was doing better and, for the sake of my mental health, I needed to be home with my family, especially my siblings. It was important to joke with my brothers and sisters, and share with them, but mostly to be part of the daily routine of life again. I was sure that the only way forward was by going home. Plus, I was sure my mental health would improve if I was with the people I loved, in surroundings that were familiar and felt safe.

Our need was publicized because the newspapers never stopped following my family's journey. So, they also made public my father's plan to uproot the family from our home to find one that would meet my needs. It seemed so unfair that my family would have to be uprooted because of me, but my father didn't see any other way. However, that was not without its own financial hardships. We weren't planning on moving, and it was just one more expense, adding to what seemed like an ever-growing list.

My father was stressed on so many levels. He would think that I didn't know, but I wasn't blind. As a man myself, I can understand the position he was in. When you have a family, you take on the responsibility of caring for them through thick and thin. It doesn't mean that you put that responsibility on anyone else. You work and you figure it out. But that doesn't mean that you don't struggle, especially when the solutions aren't easy to find and all the work in the world isn't going to fix the financial burden you are now forced to carry.

My siblings were struggling emotionally from everything that had already happened. My little sister, Brittany, was so scared initially, but my sense of humor set her mind at ease. I was still her big brother, even if I couldn't do everything I used to. But there was still the question of how much could we ask from them? How could our family survive yet another upheaval?

This was the position my father was in, and I didn't envy him. There were so many people he had to consider and weigh in his decision. But I was going to take priority, which meant more would be demanded of my family—not just by moving, but how my care would impact our family routine and the family budget. Plus, there was the costs of home-care to consider, if we chose to go that route. What would my siblings and my parents have to give up to cover these costs?

They weren't even thinking about a lifetime of my care. Just one day at a time, with the first obstacle being getting me home at all. When something this big happens, often the only way to keep from being overwhelmed is to take it one obstacle at a time.

You start to rely on your faith to keep yourself from being swamped mentally and emotionally. There are moments in life where you find yourself looking for a higher power that can give you the strength you need beyond what you have within yourself. I found myself at the end of my own physical and mental strength many times, and I know that my parents must have also had those moments too. But during those moments, something always seemed to happen that eased the pressure. It was clear that something greater than us was guiding events to assist us through these difficult times. Those moments when total strangers stepped up — those were faith strengthening and kept us moving forward.

With all this in mind, the community truly rallied around us. They saw the need and went about addressing it. Fundraisers were held to raise the money needed to remake my father's home. Hallways needed to be widened, the bathroom needed to be made handicap accessible, and I needed to be able to access the kitchen. I couldn't cook, but I still wanted to be able to eat and be with the family. Every room needed a makeover. It wasn't just a question of throwing up a ramp at the front door and being done with it.

Ultimately, we did end up selling our home and moving to another one. Part of the selling process included a makeover of our old home. The Million Dollar Makeover, which was a local reality television show, provided the much-needed makeover, which allowed my father to get top dollar for the family home during the sale. Daniel Murphy, host and interior designer, aided by over 35 volunteers, painted, and replaced carpets and flooring within just 48 hours. The real estate agent who sold our home gave up her commission, which reduced my families' fees during this process. This meant our family received even more toward the purchase of our next home.

Numerous donations, guidance, and just the understanding of our neighbors, benefited our family. A special bathroom and an elevator were part of the upgrades our new family home received. Sponsors provided me with a $16,000 wheelchair and a wheelchair accessible vehicle. Plus, there were other retrofits, with the total costing $100,000. Donations came from everywhere, and it was these efforts from the community that finally allowed me to leave rehab and come home to be with my family. This was where my mental healing was truly able to begin.

Two Durham elementary school teachers also hosted a regular charity basketball tournament, which raised funds for various causes. One year, they chose my family to receive funds from their event. It warmed my heart that the community didn't just forget my family a few weeks after the incident, but were still helpful and active on our behalf for several years.

My mother's home also needed help, so there was work done there as well. Fundraisers helped my mom to add a lift to her home, as well as a special bed for me. Ultimately, her home renovations allowed me to have my regular weekends with my mom. Another part of my normal routine was put in place, and I felt as if I had truly rejoined my family at that point, regardless of what we had to deal with to make it possible.

This is another case where divorce and having two homes made our unique situation even more unique. My parents also said it was a crazy time because so many individuals and organizations wanted to help, and it wasn't always the most coordinated. Still, it was evident that there was a lot of love and caring from our community, making things possible that my family could not have afforded to do otherwise. Not all the financial burden disappeared, but now we knew that we could survive it, and that we wouldn't be swamped as a family.

But there was also the emotional support from the community. My family was hosted for a week in Montreal, thanks to the Starlight Starbright Children's Foundation. I got to meet a few of my favorite stars from the Ultimate Fighting Championship (UFC). Plus, there was the visit from the Maple Leafs. These were moments that allowed us to be just a family and, while we couldn't forget what had happened, we could just be normal.

Still, what ended up being so helpful was meeting other people in the same boat as I was. If you haven't ever been here, you can be supportive, but it's hard to truly put yourself into my chair, so to speak. But talking to those who had been where I was, gave me such a boost. They helped me to see that a future was possible—that I could work, socialize, and have an adult life—independent of my parents. My life wasn't over, and they were living proof that I could still go out and claim an amazing life, if I was willing to work for it.

When I got home, initially, I had a full day. First, it was therapy in the morning, then I was off to school for the afternoon. The stairs impacted what classes I could attend, but they worked with me, so I could graduate. Eventually, I completed high school and received five award certificates from the Oshawa Central Collegiate Institute (OCCI).

Working with a counselor also helped me, particularly when I was dealing with a heavy bout of depression. No matter how much positive self-talk you give yourself, there are always periods when the limitations are just mentally overwhelming.

But the reality is that sometimes, I just wanted to be by myself. However, those times weren't very often, simply because I was busy, and my family wanted to be with me almost constantly. They were still getting over the scare of almost losing me. So there was a constant need to be able to touch me, look at me, talk with me, and reassure themselves that I had made it.

I was also active in plenty of community events. Before my accident, I had always thought it was every family for itself, but our community proved that wasn't the case. They made it possible for me to come home from the rehab center and gave our family an immense amount of emotional support.

If you had told me before this happened that people do things like this, I am not sure I would have believed you. Seeing what people are willing to do for one another is amazing.

Chapter Five

Starting Over at 17

Many of us don't ever see ourselves starting over at such a young age. But I was having to reimagine my life right at the time when it was just getting started. The accident had left me paralyzed from the nipples down, giving me limited control over my shoulders and arms, but definitely not the fine motor skills needed to pick up a bag or even brush my teeth. I needed help, but it just smacked against my own sense of independence.

When I first went home, I was able to operate a motorized wheelchair, but I was also dependent on two persons and a mechanical lift for transfers. I needed help with everything from eating to my bathroom needs.

My family had suffered an intense amount of strain. My step-mother had been my primary caregiver, and the stress of caring for me and the change in their lifestyle had negatively impacted their relationship. My father and step-mother ended up divorcing, as the strain of our circumstances proved to be too much for their relationship.

As any kid can, I was quick to figure out how the divorce was my fault, even though I could not have foreseen my accident in order to do anything to prevent it. Eventually, I made my peace with the divorce, and accepted that not everything in life was always going to be about me.

Then, there were my ongoing medical issues. I didn't get home and find that those issues had magically disappeared. There were the bouts with kidney stones in 2009 and 2010, which were extremely painful, plus the reality of digestive problems, and pressure ulcers. Of course, the physicians also kept assessing me but, by 2012, it was determined that my paralysis was likely permanent, and there would be no further changes in spinal cord transmission.

The strain at my father's house eventually got to be too much. You can love people very much, but it doesn't always mean that you can live with them. After a while, it was clear I needed a change of scene, and my dad needed a break.

I decided to head to my mother's. She was able to take care of me for a time, but it soon became clear that I was an extra burden at a time when she was chasing a toddler, plus mothering all of my other siblings. Her ability to juggle everything started to crack. I could see that this wasn't working for my family at all. My options seemed to be bouncing from one family member to the next, unless I could find another way.

I needed to strike out on my own. I didn't always want to be with my family, as much as I loved them and was grateful for their support. My siblings were growing up and moving on, and building their own lives. I wanted to do that too! The question was, how could I do it? Would it be possible, or would I be forced to live with my family or in an institution?

So, I came up with the idea of getting my own place. It meant that I would have to have someone assist me during the day, but I was determined that I would make it happen. I was going to live on my own and take control of my life, like any other adult would. I might have my physical limitations, but I wasn't going to let them hold me back from living to the fullest.

My first apartment wasn't a huge place, but it was big enough for me to get around in my wheelchair. I had someone come in to help me with bathing, dressing, and making my meals. At the end of the day, they would help me get settled into bed, and then I was on my own until the morning.

Those nights were incredibly difficult. I was left lying there until the morning, just staring at the ceiling. I couldn't even turn myself over or adjust my position. Imagine just staring at the ceiling all night, with nothing but your own thoughts to entertain you. In the night, my thoughts could quickly match the darkness around me, which was just mentally draining. I had to find ways to keep myself focused on the positive, however little I might find at that moment. It was that or lose my mind to depression and anxiety.

By myself, it was easy to start throwing a pity party with one attendee. I can't honestly say that I didn't have a few of those pity parties. But when you are lying in your own vomit, yelling for help, and there is nobody there to help clean you up, and you can't do it yourself, it takes a mental toll on you. I don't know that anyone could go through such a huge change in their life without having a few of those pity parties.

But in those moments, it was key to be mentally tough with myself. I needed to tell myself that I could forge a life for myself, and it was possible to reach goals that I set for myself. It might not be what I originally had planned, but my life was definitely not over! I reminded myself that God wouldn't have helped me come so far if he didn't think I had more to contribute to the world.

One of the benefits of living on my own was learning what jobs and careers were available to me. After all, it wasn't like I could do some of the more traditionally physical jobs. I couldn't swing a hammer, for instance; although, if I tried, and hit my own thumb, I wasn't likely to feel it. But technology opened up a new wave of opportunities for me—I could still talk and use a voice-activated computer; I could send emails; and give detailed instructions that would produce documents and even drawings.

To go to school, receive training, and go to work like anyone else was huge for me. I wasn't just stuck at home in a bed or my wheelchair. I was going out into the world. I was engaging and become a productive member of society, just like anyone else. That was a huge mental and emotional lift for me.

Being on my own meant I was back in charge of my own social life too. Living with my folks, it was hard to make plans to go out with my friends and be a teenager. They worried about so many of the details of getting me from point A to B, that they missed the point of going out. It was to socialize as a person, not as a quadriplegic.

I remember hanging out with friends on one occasion and mentioning that I needed to go to the bathroom. My friend asked what I needed him to do, and I told him I would need him to hold it up while I peed. He was completely willing but looked relieved when I told him that really all anyone had to do was empty my collection bag, because I had a catheter.

Joking with my friends like that was so important to my well-being and mental health. It made me feel like one of the guys again—just a normal guy. That feeling wasn't always easy to achieve but, every time I did, it felt like I reclaimed a part of my life again. I was staking claim to my right to live and contribute to the world. I wasn't a burden, and it was so critical to my overall mental well-being to remember that.

Other parts of my life were starting to come together as well. I was dating and trying to find the one. I refused to deny myself the joy of a loving partner just because I couldn't move the way I had before. My focus was finding my happiness and staking claim to it. From a personal point of view, I was making the leap from child to adult.

That meant making choices for myself, not giving those choices to others and using my accident as a reason to be a victim the rest of my life. But deep inside, I was still dealing with depression and anxiety. After all, if I made a decision, I still needed people to help me carry it out. So, if someone disagrees with you, it wasn't like I could just walk out and do it anyway.

One thing that my accident taught me was how to communicate with others effectively. After all, I need to be able to ask others to help me with the basics of living; coming across as demanding rarely works to motivate people to want to help you. Plus, I have to learn how to separate my needs for a caregiver from the other aspects of my relationships, including my romantic ones. I am not always a patient, and I need to remind myself of that from time to time.

We all have the right to live a life of purpose and happiness. But we need to be active in finding our purpose and creating our happiness. They won't just come to you. Envision your life but, remember, without some action on your part, your vision will remain just that.

No matter who you are, we all have the ability to dig down deep and find a well of strength we didn't even know we had, so that we can get through the toughest situations and circumstances that could swamp us, mentally and physically. I had to find that well of strength much earlier than anyone could have imagined.

I could have spent my life in bed, staring at the ceiling, but I chose to get out in the world and build a life. I changed how I thought about what was possible and found out that my life truly wasn't over. Yes, it had changed, but it wasn't over. My physical limitations didn't define my world—I did. And I decided to define it differently than the doctors, or even my family. I decided to thrive, not just survive.

That wasn't easy. I was, and still am, at risk for multiple secondary health complications. These include skin breakdown, neurogenic "burning" pain in the shoulders and upper back, involuntary spasms of the legs and trunk, osteoporosis, premature coronary artery disease, increased risk of pulmonary infections, and likely future episodes of autonomic dysreflexia, which is a potentially life threatening condition characterized by dangerously high blood pressure elevations.

Plus, I had to have the help of my caregivers to make sure that my skin doesn't breakdown. If that breakdown was to occur, it could develop sores and could lead to infections that I would be unlikely to easily recover from. Prevention was important because my pressure ulcers had shown how dangerous a wound could be.

Additionally, there are those day to day realities of needing help to get transferred to my wheelchair, in and out of bed, and also with the many aspects of bathing and grooming.

It also meant that it was hard to be spontaneous, and the reality was that my injury presented an ongoing challenge to all the activities that I wanted to pursue, including educational, work, and recreation. They were possible, but it meant that there was plenty of extra planning that had to go into everything I did. That hasn't changed at all in the years since.

I also get tired easily, which means I need to plan out my activities to avoid exhausting myself. Among so many things that were hard to accept, having limited energy to do what I wanted was one of the worst. It also meant that in choosing my career, I was going to have to take into account my inability to work long hours.

Have you ever heard the expression that the loss of one sense can mean your remaining senses are sharpened? I don't know if that is completely true, but I do believe my appreciation of life was sharpened by the loss of my mobility and most of my sense of touch. It would be so easy to get down about my situation, but I find myself actively looking for things to appreciate and be grateful for. It helps me to keep my head focused on the positive.

But I don't want to tell you that it is always easy. There are days when the depression and anxiety of my situation overwhelm me. It's like being a boat when a large wave comes by. Sometimes the boat can ride it out with no trouble but, at other times, the boat gets swamped by the wave, and everyone ends up in the water. Depression is like that for me. Some days, I can ride it out; but other days, I just feel as if I am underwater.

Fighting this feeling and coming back to the surface, so to speak, requires a lot of effort on my part. But having people around me who are supportive and willing to listen, definitely helps. I also make an effort to get out of the house. Since I am able to work from home, it can be easy to stay put and not get out. But socializing is key to getting out of my own head.

When you are with others, it is harder to dwell on what isn't going right in your own life. Instead, you naturally start to focus on others. My sense of humor has also survived this experience. I was funny and quick to try to get a laugh or smile from just about anyone, and that really hasn't changed. However, now when I get someone to laugh or smile, it helps them to not dwell on my circumstances, and just to get to know me as a person.

When I was in the hospital so many years ago, my joking and laughing reassured my little sister that everything would be alright. People often feel uncomfortable at first because they don't want to make me feel uncomfortable. They also don't know how to always address the elephant in the room, which means I feel obligated at times to help them get past the wheelchair and what it implies.

Here is where I have to tell you a truth about having such an obvious physical disability. It can be difficult to just get people to see you for who you are, when it isn't easy for them to see past all the gear that comes with being a quadriplegic. Then there are those moments when you wonder if people want to spend time with you because of your personality, or because they feel sorry for you.

It's a particular challenge that comes into play in romantic relationships. You recognize that they are going to have to do more for you than they would in other relationships because of the physical assistance you will need throughout your life. Plus, many of the jobs that would be considered *man's work* (taking out the trash, for instance), I just can't do. If my girlfriend needs a jar opened, she can't just call me into the kitchen to pop it open. It makes it necessary to set some ground rules early in any relationship. But once you do, it is amazing how you really get to know the different sides of an individual. It is key to taking a relationship to the next, deeper level. And it was also the key to finding the person who makes my life complete and is truly my angel.

Chapter Six

Finding Love and More

My girlfriend, at the time of my accident, stayed with me until I was in rehab. Once it was obvious that I was never going to walk on my own again, I gave her the choice to stay or go. She went. I can't really blame her because it was a tough situation for me to go through and she was just 15 herself.

If I had never had the accident, would we have been a forever love, married after school, and had a family of our own? I doubt it. The truth is, most of us don't end up with a high school sweetheart. Plus, our relationship was young and didn't have a foundation to deal with all the trauma and stress that my accident brought down on it. We were too young to make those kind of forever commitments. I understand that now but, at the time, I was just hurt. Breakups are never easy, but they are worse when you have nothing to do but dwell on them for hours on end while you wait to go to rehab, or for your next visitor.

While I understood why she didn't stick around, I admit that I wondered if any woman would. By society's standards, I wasn't a whole man anymore. It meant there was a real possibility that I wouldn't be able to have children or even a physically intimate relationship with a woman. Coming to terms with that would be hard for a grown adult, let alone a young man who wasn't even out of high school yet.

Getting out and socializing was key to meeting the woman of my dreams. Like many guys, I love anything that goes fast. I can definitely get that wheelchair zooming when I want to. Zooming around at a local business, I met someone who would profoundly impact my life.

Kara

I met Mike when he was zooming past me at work. I immediately thought he was cute. I didn't have a chance to say hi that day because he was just gone in a flash. At this point, the thought that he was in a wheelchair didn't even factor into it. He was just a cute guy who looked like he might be fun to hang out with.

A few days later, he finally slowed down enough to notice me, stopping to say hi and tell me how cute I was. We instantly hit it off and I found myself excited to talk with him again. We exchanged numbers, and our relationship grew from there.

One of the best things about Mike is his outgoing personality. You just can't be down when you are around him. He is so funny and not afraid to tell you what he thinks. That bold personality drew me to him. We started hanging out more and more. The bond was starting to form, but there were some initial reservations on his side about putting his heart and soul into the relationship. After all, our life is not always easy.

Our relationship was growing and deepening, but the reality of Mike's injury does have an impact on our lives and adds unique challenges that average couples probably don't face. Being part of Mike's life means helping him with various activities throughout the day. It isn't like Mike can just grab his phone or shrug off his sweatshirt. The smallest everyday tasks often require an extra set of hands, and those are mine.

I remember one instance not long into our relationship when Mike asked me to help him take off his sweater. I tried, but quickly gave up, telling Mike it was too hard. He got mad and told me to go if I couldn't help him. With that choice in front of me, I realized how much I cared for him. I didn't want to leave. So, I tried again and, this time, we got the sweater off.

Then we had a long talk, and Mike explained that being with him wasn't going to be a cakewalk. It was going to involve a lot of tasks throughout the day that I would have to help him with. If I wasn't willing to help him, then our relationship wasn't going to work out in the long run. It was the reality of Mike's life that he needed someone with a truly generous and giving personality.

Have you ever had an experience where someone brought out the best in you? Someone who helps you see what you can be and just adds so much to your life? Mike is one of those people in my life. He made me feel differently than any other guy had. I realized that the way he made me feel was worth holding on to. I was willing to push through all the obstacles to give him everything that he needed, because we both benefited in the long run. I realized that my needs were also being met, particularly emotionally and mentally.

There was also a huge learning curve for me. I didn't have any traditional medical training, and I had never had to care for anyone in this way before. But Mike was patient with me because I think he knew that I really wanted to help. I got a handle on the routine, but I also earned something else that I value even more—his trust. Nowadays, you could call me Dr. Kara!

But Mike wasn't the only one whose trust I had to earn. Mike's family was big and had been through a lot during the accident and the new reality of Mike's paralysis. They were very protective because they didn't want to see him get hurt. I knew I wasn't going to hurt him because I was falling in love with him, but it took a while to convince them.

The only time Mike and I got into a confrontation was when he played a cruel but romantic prank on me to test my limits. When I got home, he told me to pack up all my stuff and leave. I couldn't understand why when I thought everything was going good. I ended up packing all my stuff, emotionally distraught. I was ready to leave when Mike made a comment saying he pissed himself, and he asked if I would mind giving him a hand before I left. Little did I know, that wasn't the case, but I didn't hesitate to help, even when I was so emotional and upset with him. I was beginning to check when a box popped out of his pants. I asked, "What is that?" He told me to open it. To my surprise, it was a white gold diamond chain with a heart in the middle of the circle, and he told me that no matter what happens between us, he will always love me.

Mom (Loretta)

After Michael's accident, I admit that I became extremely protective. I had seen him so helpless in that bed, fighting for his life, and it was hard to imagine that he would be able to care for himself in the world without us. But Michael proved us wrong, leaving home and figuring it out on his own. Still, I saw the reality that someone could take advantage of him. He is such a generous and caring guy. My fear was that people might use him and then leave him, which would be a horrible experience for him emotionally.

I just wasn't sure that he was up to it. So, anytime a girl came around, she was immediately under the gun and given the 5th degree. I guess I let my worry cloud my judgement at times because, to be honest, there weren't any girls that I really liked. Then, Kara showed up. I didn't like her at first. I figured she was just enjoying the novelty of dating a guy in a wheelchair, and that she would end up leaving when the shine of the relationship wore off. That would have been devastating for

Michael, and would bring out the protective momma bear in me. There was also the deeper worry that someone could come along and physically abuse him, which was something I was aware of constantly. I worried over every bruise, trying to make sure that he wasn't being hurt in that way.

I wanted to strike first, before he was far too invested emotionally or was damaged physically. I told him to get rid of her and move on. Kara definitely had a rough time at first. There was no question she was going to have to prove she was willing to stick around. Our family gave her a heck of a hazing. I thought for sure she would be gone in a flash.

But we didn't deter her. She loved him, and I finally had to realize that she wasn't going anywhere. It took me a while to warm up to her, but the way she helped Michael and took care of him really helped me to see what a wonderful woman she was. Her love for my son was shown through her actions, and it was clear that he was completely in love as well.

Kara

Once his family's trust was earned, they really opened up to me and drew me into the fold. They felt confident that I was really in love with Mike, and they didn't have to worry that I wasn't going to give him anything but the best possible care, love, and support.

I have been asked many times what draws me to Mike. While this is a question I am sure every couple is asked, it stands out more for us because people often just see Mike's paralysis, and they tend to stop right there. So, my answer is from the heart, but it also draws their attention back to who Mike really is and his awesome personality.

Mike attracts me because he makes me feel like I am on top of the world, and no one is more special than me. Even after all our years together, Mike still can make me feel like no one else is more important. He is always willing to show me how much he loves me, even out in public, when most guys seem to clam up. He is smart, funny, and a bit of a smart-ass, but it just draws me to him. Not to mention he is a great-looking guy. He's the whole package, and it wouldn't matter if he was walking or not.

But don't get me wrong; we still have moments where we struggle, but I don't know anyone who manages to have a relationship with no bumps in the road. Plus, we have the added reality of Mike's situation. He lost so much at such a young age. As a result, he still battles with depression and anxiety. I don't blame him for those feelings, and I support him during those dark times. I recognize that this is our reality; it is a never-ending process of accepting his situation for what it is, while still finding ways to grow as a person, in spite of the physical challenges.

What I love about Mike is the fact that during the worst times of his life, when he really just hates his situation, he refuses to give up. He is motivated to always better himself and others. I remember one time when he went to Little Caesar's and bought $100 worth of $5 pizzas. Then he took them to the food bank. It is his generous nature that appeals to so many people, but it is just one more thing that I love about him.

There is a natural part of Mike that recognizes he has a larger part to play in this world, and that his contribution isn't limited by his physical challenges; I think it has only enhanced his empathy for others. He has also gone beyond the surface of just living life, to living life to the fullest. This includes exploring the spiritual side of his nature. He can't hide behind his physical abilities, like so many individuals do, and ignore the reality of something deeper and greater. His accident brought him face to face with a higher power, with God. How else could you explain his survival? We can't accomplish everything on our own power. Mike is truly an example of what faith, love, and generosity can accomplish.

He puts a smile on everyone's face, but none bigger than the one he puts on mine on a daily basis.

Mike

Kara is my angel. There is no other way to describe it. When I met her, I just saw a cute girl. But as I got to know her, I couldn't help but be drawn to her spirit. It was loving and generous. When I had that intense conversation with her about what being my girlfriend was going to entail, I really thought that would be the end of the relationship. It isn't easy to be in a relationship with me. How many couples have to deal with the realities of paralysis throughout their entire lives?

But she takes it in stride. It's our life, and she makes it the best it could be. I know there are days when I am struggling emotionally, but she just keeps going. She is truly my rock.

As a couple, we also decided that we wanted to have a family of our own. I am an uncle many times over, and I love kids. I can be so silly, and kids are just drawn to someone who makes them giggle. But even this part of my life was challenging.

Chapter Seven

Building a Family

Kara and I, like any couple, had multiple discussions about starting a family. Part of my paralysis is that I didn't necessarily have the normal type of control over my lower body, and it impacted my ability to have children. When you are 15 and struggling for your life, whether or not you can have kids seems to be almost an afterthought.

But in your twenties, when you are in love with a wonderful woman, the reality of not being able to have kids becomes a real challenge. I didn't want to not have a family, and I knew Kara would make an amazing mother. The question was, how were we going to create our family?

In this day and age, there are more options than ever before. Twenty years or more ago, I wouldn't have necessarily survived, let alone been able to have a family of my own. The medical advances have been incredible, giving us more options than we thought possible.

But there are also the real-life obstacles of trying to build a family with my medical challenges. While adoption was a potential route, there were also issues about how I could handle parenthood. The hoops would have been extensive for me. Having a baby naturally would eliminate jumping through those hoops to prove our fitness to be parents, but having a baby naturally would be a trick.

Kara and I did our homework and came up with IVF as an option for moving forward to have a baby of our own. This was going to allow us to have a baby that was part of me and part of her. Our own child, with our unique characteristics. But it was also going to be asking a lot of Kara, who was going to need to be physically poked and prodded, not to mention the hormones.

The reality is that couples can fall apart over the stress of having a baby. Not getting pregnant right away and having multiple failed tries can add a level of stress that wears a relationship down. We refused to believe it wouldn't be successful, but I also knew that at some point, we may have to face the possibility that children weren't going to be part of our future. I worried and prayed about growing our family because I wasn't sure how not being able to grow in this direction as a couple could impact our long-term relationship. Questions flooded through my mind, but I kept them at bay, determined to see this through with Kara, whatever it might bring.

Kara

IVF isn't a guarantee of anything. You could do it multiple times and still have nothing more than the dream of a child. Plus, we had to be approved to even try. But we were successful in getting the funding approved. Our first try was a disappointment because we didn't get pregnant.

That was an emotional toll because you can't help but get your hopes up, only to have them dashed with a negative pregnancy test. Then you can't help but wonder if you will ever get pregnant. For me, there were thoughts of what I might have done wrong. Should I have rested more? Did I lift something I shouldn't have? The internal doubts just don't seem to give you a rest, mentally or emotionally.

Then you find yourself almost obsessing about ovulation dates, implantation, and viable embryos for the procedures. Medical intervention to get pregnant is not only a financial expense; it also takes an emotional and mental toll. You can be warned about the difficulties of that experience, but you can't really appreciate how intense it is until you are the couple in the middle of tests, hormone shots, and intense waiting periods to hear from doctors about embryo viability and test results.

Even when you try to take your mind off of it, you can't help but find yourself drawn to all the babies you see in public. Then there are days where it is just too hard to see a baby, while the uncertainty of whether you will hold one of your own hangs over your head.

Our second round, however, took us to the other end of the emotional spectrum: pure joy! We found out that we were pregnant, with our baby due July 2017. The emotional highs and lows of the first round were forgotten as we started planning for the arrival of our little one. I can't wait to see Mike as a dad. He is so good with kids, and I think it is because he is still a kid at heart. Our child will be blessed with two amazing parents who love him/her. At the same time, they will be blessed with the opportunity to grow up being more understanding and empathic for those who are different, or face unique physical challenges.

Our life will be fuller, but I also understand that more will be expected of me physically. I will need to give the extra hugs that Mike won't necessarily be able to. I will be the one picking them up and checking for boo-boos after they fall. Mike won't be able to teach them how to ride a bike or climb a tree. But he will be able to impart far more important lessons.

I see my child being more loving because they will see the example that we set with each other. They will see that a physical disability doesn't have to define a person, but that there are so many more aspects to who you are as a person. Physical attributes don't compare to how you treat others, how you deal with tragedy, how you face difficult situations with courage, or how you remain positive throughout all of life's ups and downs.

When you reach the point of parenthood, you have grand dreams about how you will raise your child and for their future. It doesn't always mean that they come together the way you plan, but if you come from a place of love, the future will always be bright in the end. Now that I am almost a mother, I have a deeper understanding of what Mike's parents must have gone through all those years ago as they watched Mike fight for his life. They had to grieve the future they thought their son would have, and embrace the new possibilities that his life had to offer. It is a lot to take in. As a parent, you clearly go through a roller coaster of emotions during the life of your child. I am at the beginning, but it is a journey that I am excited to begin with my life partner.

Mike

I wonder, after this little one is born, if we will try again. There are no guarantees that we would have another successful round of IVF. This could be our only little miracle. But I would be okay with that, because this little miracle is so precious to me. We talk about names, our dreams for this child, and what we imagine their future might be like.

Do I think about my child wrestling? I admit that I do from time to time. I still don't know if I will say no when the time comes. I don't want my fears from my experiences to stop them from exploring sports and the joys that come with that. But then again, no one expected my accident and life-altering injury from one wrestling match either.

So it will have to be discussed, and I am sure that Kara will help me to overcome my fears and doubts. We are a team; she helps me immensely with the mental wounds of my injury every day.

Last Match

    I am grateful for my partner, my child, and my ability to spend time with them both. It is a blessing I didn't know if I would ever have, the day I stepped onto the mat for the last time in 2007.

Chapter Eight

Where Do I Go From Here?

I ask myself this question a lot. I don't want to be sitting on my sorrows. There is so much to do and explore in this life that I can't imagine not conquering something else. I hear about new experiments that are helping patients like myself regain mobility through a variety of innovative devices. I won't lie; the kid in me is intrigued by the various gadgets that remind me of a video game controller.

Every time I hear about another medical breakthrough, I can't help but have a little hope that I could have some of my own mobility restored. It would be so nice to move about on my own, even if it was just transferring myself from my wheelchair to the couch without help.

But even if I never achieve the ability to walk, or even have increased mobility again, I won't have any regrets. It is because I have built this life for myself. I have struggled against the darkest hours, and I have come through stronger mentally, emotionally, and spiritually. I might have my scars, but I also have my life, and it is a good one. I have people to live for and experiences that I know have made my life richer and unique.

Would I have had that same rich life without my accident? It is impossible to say what I would have done had the situation turned out differently, but I believe in my heart that I was always going to live to the fullest; my personality couldn't let me do otherwise.

Every once in a while, I get asked if Kara and I are going to get married. I personally don't feel the desire to showcase my commitment to Kara in such a public fashion, but I recognize that others do feel this is a necessary step in their relationship. I leave it open-ended, as I don't know how I might feel about taking that kind of step in a few years.

My life has more of a day by day feeling, and that makes it hard for me to plan too far into the future. I understand that nothing is guaranteed. Just because you woke up today, doesn't mean that you are going to wake up tomorrow. Every day that I spent in that hospital, fighting for my life and my sanity, taught me to appreciate the gift I have of being able to still contribute to the lives of others in a meaningful way.

It isn't always easy to move forward, especially when I am having a bad day and the frustration mounts because I can't do something on my own. I am sure that I owe Kara a few *I'm sorry(s)* for the days when I take my frustrations out on her. But I appreciate that she doesn't hold it against me, and recognizes that I needed to vent and knows how much I love and appreciate her.

Our new addition is also about to change our lives in a profound way. As a father, I understand that I will be helping to shape a new little life. But the way that my father was able to play with me and be physical will not be part of our relationship. So this will be a new territory, and it won't be as though I can just run to my parents for advice. They have never been in this situation either. But it is going to be an amazing experience, and I am ready to embrace it, even with all the challenges and unique obstacles that it will present.

Does that mean I will miss changing a diaper? Okay, I have to be honest, that part I won't miss as much, but I don't know too many dads standing in that line, eagerly awaiting the first poopy diaper to change. Thanks to having a loving partner, though, I will be able to snuggle with my child, because Kara will help me. I also have the ability to converse, reason, and get to know the heart of my kid. You don't need legs and arms to do that.

Life will be full of joy, but I know there will be messy parts. The gift of life is being able to embrace all the mess and extract all the good and loving aspects from it. Life takes work and action on our part, but the best lives are ones where individuals actively engage, versus just coasting through.

Another part of my life that continues to grow is my ability to explore my spirituality. I can study a variety of religions, but I also have the ability to meditate, pray, and contemplate the deeper questions of life. I survived for a reason, and I want to make sure that I am not missing my life's purpose because I am feeling sorry for myself.

When you meditate, you take a moment to connect with yourself on a deeper level. It's also a great way to connect with your spiritual side because you can take time to speak with your God or higher power. As you allow your spiritual side to grow, it can be a source of strength and control. I wouldn't always have said that in the past, but I now recognize that there is more to this life than physical strength and ability. There are the deeper things of the heart, mind, and soul, and they can't be found just anywhere.

I also have to take time to reflect on what got me here. Wrestling was one of my great joys because it allowed me to exert my physical ability around others. It gave me a sense of achievement, and I used it to define who I was as a person. Once it was gone, I found myself having to figure out who I was all over again. I know that I am not the only one who has ever had to dig deep and find new meaning in his life. Others have faced these types of challenges, but I found that my search led me to a deeper understanding of others, as well as myself.

I learned that people get scared for their loved ones, and that it doesn't always bring out the best in them at every moment. But I also learned that people have the ability to do the most profound things out of love for a fellow human, even one that they have never met. There are moments of profound tragedy, but there are also amazing moments of grace, which can help us down the roughest roads.

My parents also showed me what true love really is. They both never stopped giving me the support I needed to rebuild my life. Both were willing to make huge sacrifices to stand by me and help me with whatever I needed. There was no obstacle that they weren't willing to help me overcome. I couldn't ask for a better example to follow as I embark on my own parenting journey.

Today, it is clear that I have moved beyond what doctors initially thought was possible. I have found a way to work, continued my education, found the love of my life, started my own family, and have begun to tentatively plan for the future. I know that I might not live as long as someone without my unique physical limitations, but that doesn't mean I can't live a full life, with a breadth of experiences and memories.

There are people around the world who are so busy working and focusing on what they are achieving professionally, that they don't take the time to appreciate what they already have personally. They end up cheating themselves out of a full life, one rich with experiences, because they don't take the time to explore all that life has to offer. I lost the ability to move on my own, but I have that full life because I take the time to explore and experience as much as possible.

No one ever reaches the end of their life saying they wish that they had worked more. I learned that lesson when I was far younger than most people, but it is one that we all need to take to heart.

I hope I have inspired you to take time to appreciate the blessings in your life. After all, you never know when something life-altering can happen. Especially when you are 15, and they call the start of a wrestling match. All you can do is be ready to rise to the challenge. "Ready, set, wrestle!"

About the Author

Mike Box is an author, graphic artist, business partner for Key Haulage, and a musician, as well as looking into creating technology. He lives in Canada, along with his partner, Kara. He continues to remain close to his family and continues to work to stay healthy. Mike is expecting his first child, Logan, in July 2017.